Free Yourself!

Archbishop Q.S. Caldwell

BK Royston Publishing
http://www.bkroystonpublishing.com
bkroystonpublishing@gmail.com

© 2024

All Rights Reserved. No part of this book may be reproduced, stored in a retrieval system, or transmitted by any means without the written permission of the author.

Cover Design: iCreate LLC

ISBN-13: 978-1-963136-00-5

Amplified Bible (AMP) Copyright © 2015 by The Lockman Foundation, La Habra, CA 90631. All rights reserved.

King James Version (KJV) - Public Domain

New International Version (NIV) - Holy Bible, New International Version®, NIV® Copyright ©1973, 1978, 1984, 2011 by Biblica, Inc.® Used by permission. All rights reserved worldwide. NIV Reverse Interlinear Bible: English to Hebrew and English to Greek. Copyright © 2019 by Zondervan.

Printed in the United States of America

TABLE OF CONTENTS

FOREWORD(s)
Pastor Jacob R. Arreola   v
Archbishop Eugene James Blount   vi

Tributes
Mother Marie A.P. Bohannon   viii
Bishop Christopher Zebedee Dowtin III   ix

Dedication to Sons and Daughter   x

Chapter 1   1
Isolation Is Insulation!

Chapter 2   17
Ignore The Noise!

Chapter 3   43
Positioned In A Place to Save!

Chapter 4   59
Confrontation VS. Confirmation –
Deliverance from Rejection

Final Thoughts   **111**

References   **158**

FOREWORD

The catastrophes we face in life rarely result from what we see or experience on the surface. Rather, many, if not most of the time, our struggles, stand-stills, and sore spots are the result of much deeper traumas, triggers, and issues. In his newest book, entitled "*Free Yourself*!" Archbishop Q.S. Caldwell strategically intertwines the wisdom of personal life experience, extensive educational insight, and biblical revelation knowledge throughout, in an attempt to confront whatever has held you back. Whether you are a pastor, CEO, educator, student, or stay-at-home parent, prepare yourself to be both challenged (for the sake of your freedom) and empowered (for the sake of your purpose), all at the same time!

-Jacob Arreola, Pastor of Calvary Church

Fort Worth, Texas; President of Jacob R. Arreola Ministries Inc.

Archiepiscopal Offices

of
His Eminence

The Most Reverend Eugene J. Blount Primate

The International Fellowship of Elim

FOREWORD
By
Archbishop Eugene James Blount

Archbishop Q. S. Caldwell is a man of great faith. For more than four decades he has consistently maintained an unparalleled heart for ministry. His love for God is evidenced by his Christian walk. His belief and trust in The Lord to produce miracles is conspicuous. In fact, he himself is a living and walking miracle. One of his favorite sayings for years has been, "Don't Breakdown Before Your Breakthrough." Hence, his latest work of ministry in written form, entitled, Free Yourself!

In this compelling, compassionate and comprehensive work, Archbishop Q. S. Caldwell brings it home. He outlines both a path and a process to free yourself. By the use of biblical text, carefully selected biblical characters, and practical steps for application, he shows us that the journey to a breakthrough can happen. Interestingly, while reading the book, I found myself reflecting on when I needed to be liberated. Thus, "Free Yourself" is a reminder to me of what God did for me. Likewise, every reader will become engaged and focused on the powerful ability of God. After all, with God all things are possible!

In conclusion, I congratulate my friend and colleague on producing an exceptional work. "Free Yourself" is straight to the point. It is a necessary tool for every individual, household, and even small groups, especially in the trying times in which we now live. I highly recommend this great work by Archbishop Q. S. Caldwell.

Best,
Eugene Blount

The Most Reverend Eugene James Blount,
Archbishop Primate, The Elim International Fellowship Brooklyn, New York

FOREVER IN OUR HEARTS

Mother
Marie A.P. Bohannon

WHO CAN FIND A VIRTUOUS WOMAN
FOR HER PRICE IS FAR ABOVE RUBIES
PROVERBS 31:10-31
KING JAMES VERSION

Mother Marie A.P. Bohannon was a true woman of God that was graced with a timeless elegance and a Spirit of intercession.

We are grateful for her life and ministry. Mother Bohannon served in the ministry for many years, and she made a significant impact on the lives of many women. She was a loving and compassionate leader with zeal, charisma, and grace.

She was a woman of great value, and she will be remembered for her legacy of strength, courage, and leadership.

General Supervisor of Women
Celebration of Praise Ministries, Inc.
4th In Succession

ARCHBISHOP Q.S. CALDWELL, TH.D., D.D.
Presiding Bishop & Chief Apostle Celebration of Praise Ministries,

Memory Eternal

BISHOP SAINT CHRISTOPHER ZEBEDEE DOWTIN, III

12.14.1973 – 04.7.2020

Bishop Saint Christopher Zebedee Dowtin, III served in the ministry for many years, and he made a significant impact on the lives of many people. He was a loving and compassionate pastor, and he always put the needs of others before his own. He was also a bold and courageous evangelist, and he never shied away from sharing the gospel message. When you reached out to me and asked me to be your father, I did not know that I was embracing such a "gentle giant" that was so encouraging and kept me motivated to continue forward in my journey. I do miss the early morning calls to make sure my rest was well and the late night calls to ensure that my day was prosperous. There are times when the Lord will allow a son or a daughter to be birthed into your life and then there are sons and daughters that God will give to you that will be an enhancement to your life. I will always cherish and remember the blessing that he was to me.

Bishop Dowtin was a true man of God, and he will be deeply missed by all who knew him.
We are grateful for his life and ministry, and we know that he is now present with the Father.
The Bible says that a good man leaves an inheritance to his children's children (Proverbs 13:22).
He has left us a rich inheritance of faith, love, and courage. We will never forget him, and we will continue to be inspired by his example.

We know that we will see him again one day, and we look forward to that day with great anticipation.

ARCHBISHOP Q.S. CALDWELL, TH.D., D.D.
Presiding Bishop & Chief Apostle Celebration of Praise Ministries, Inc.

A DEDICATION
To Sons & Daughter

Prophetess Atavia Barnes
To my Daughter, who is an Author of multiple books, that dedicated her 1st Book to me.
The honor was truly overwhelming.
Over the years, I have watched you grow up in the Ministry and see you successfully embrace your purpose. Your grandmother, who was my very first Church Mother at Joy Temple of Lenox, brought you to me broken but you were willing to be discipled.
Seeing where you are now encourages me to keep Imparting because my "Product is still Producing."

Bishop John "Jock" Lester
Life is never boring with you around. From aggravating me a playing pranks on me as only you can. Our relationship can summed up by the sentiments of God towards Jesus in Matt 3:17 - "This is my beloved Son, in whom I am well pleased. Watching you grow from a "little fella" to the man that you h become today is a testament that impartation is impactful. many people tell me that watching you Minister is a reminde myself.
I said some years ago, your presence is equals to the strengtl 10 sons. You are a great example of faithfulness, loyalty, an commitment. Favor will always be your friend!

Dr. Robert O'Keefe Hassell
I am appreciative for the continued Honor that you bestow upon me that is genuine and intentional.
It is truly an Enhancement to my Movement.

Even with you being an Author of multiple books, you continue to bug me about my Sermon notes. Our conversations bring inspiration and revelation that frequently turn into messages of hope that are invaluable.
Because of you, I'll never be empty.

Prophet Brandon D. Howard
To the One that Loves to pick my brain and continues to kee me encouraged with motivational and inspirational Words th will never be forgotten.
Your actions remind me of how Elisha pursued Elijah because are always close.

Brandon, your Place of Covering is an Avenue to Receiving. Eli would not leave until he had received. Stay Focused and eve Deposit will Position you for continued blessings.

Chapter 1

Isolation Is Insulation!

Psalm 27:10 (KJV) - When my father and my mother forsake me, then the Lord will take me up.

Psalm 27 is merely entitled A David Psalm. As with the collection of David's psalms, it is impossible to say with certainty when this one was composed. It speaks of conflict with enemies, adversaries, false witnesses, and violent men, but this was a recurring theme throughout King David's existence. There is such a drastic difference between the first and second halves of this psalm that scholars believe it is a composite of two separate psalms.

David penned Psalm 27 during a period of intense trial and doubt. David admits to feeling anxious and frightened in the psalm, but he also proclaims his faith in God. At the outset of the psalm, David professes his belief in God. When asked who he should be afraid of, he replies, *A Psalm of David. The LORD is my light and my salvation; whom shall I fear? the LORD is the strength of my life; of whom shall I be afraid?* (Psalm 27:1, KJV). This is an inspiring confession of faith that reveals David's trust in God even in the face of his fears. David continues by elaborating on the difficulties he's encountering. The verse reads, *"When the wicked, even mine enemies and my foes, came upon me to eat up my flesh, they stumbled and fell"* (Psalm 27:2, KJV). This points to David being attacked, either physically or spiritually. He feels trapped and threatened, yet he trusts that God will save him.

Next, David discusses his longing to offer praise to God. His one and only desire is to spend eternity in God's presence, as expressed in Psalm 27:4. This proves that David's belief in God is not merely academic but also emotional and sincere. The only thing he wants more than anything is to be in God's loving and powerful presence.

David concludes the psalm by proclaiming his faith in God's eventual deliverance from his foes. Even so, he declares, *"I had fainted, unless I had believed to see the goodness of the LORD in the land of the living"* (Psalm 27:13, KJV). This hopeful proclamation reveals David's firm faith in God's final victory over wickedness. Psalm 27 is a constant reminder that God is our shield, our deliverer, and our fortress. He will protect us from harm at all times and never leave us alone. David understood that God's love and concern transcended even the most intimate human bonds. David likely did not anticipate that his parents would abandon him, but even if they did, God would not.

Understanding the Role of Isolation

Seasons of solitude and isolation can actually foster significant spiritual and personal growth. All of us have endured a number of extended periods of solitude and isolation. Depending on the state of our hearts during each season, we have had both negative and positive experiences. We must actively see recurring patterns in those seasons such as bitterness, sadness, depression, self-pity, anxiety, worry, and despair. If left unchecked, this can lead to destructive behavior and mistakes we will regret after a difficult moment has passed. Negative behavior is a deterrent that temporarily satisfies desires rather than waiting for God to answer. The results of giving in under these types of pressures cause injury and severe suffering. In turn, we can push others away, become self-loathing, turn inward, lack self-awareness of issues that are to our detriment, and not embrace a promising future.

These periods, in our lives, can be extremely painful and broken, but they can also be filled with profound joy and closeness with the Lord. Some of our greatest times of spiritual growth and development come to us during periods when God literally removes everything else from our lives, leaving only us and Him. This season, along with others like it, serves a purpose. When we look to Him and turn to Him during those times, He uses it to develop us!

Isolation can be challenging and lonely, but it can also be a time of tremendous growth. When we are alone, we are compelled to confront our own thoughts and emotions. We must develop both self-reliance and faith in God. God employs isolation to grow us in part by allowing us time to reflect on our lives. When we are not continuously bombarded by the noise of the world and others, we can take a step back and gain a clearer perspective on our lives. We are able to find the areas in which we need to develop and alter. Isolation can also be a period of tremendous spiritual development and self-improvement. We have the opportunity to focus on our relationship with God when we are alone and become aware of critical areas in our lives that demands attention.

Isolation and Alteration

Change can also occur during times of isolation. When we are forced to confront our own flaws, we are more likely to make positive life changes. Changing our attitudes, behaviors, or relationships may be necessary.

Change can be challenging, but it is often necessary for development. When we are receptive to change, we create opportunities for the future. We can become the individuals God intended for us to be.

Isolation and Metamorphosis

Isolation can be a transformative period. Transformation is rarely simple. It can be a difficult procedure. However, it is a necessary method for enhancement. When we allow our experiences to transform us, we get new perspectives and embody honed capabilities that allow us to do things that we have never done before. Isolation can be a challenging experience, but it can also be a time of tremendous growth, conversion, and adjustment. When we are willing to confront the difficulties of isolation, we can appear more robust and complete.

Isolation, at times, can put us in a mental place where we feel forsaken. However, purpose is often discovered in isolation and manifested potential is realized during moments of crisis. Isolation is an opportunity for deep self-discovery. Isolation positions us for our purpose, initiates the processes of training and proving us for the assignment that lies ahead of us. Isolation does not mean we have been abandoned. Refuse to develop a disposition of abandonment because of temporary isolation. Dwelling on abandonment will rob you of the opportunities to embrace impartation.

David was the eighth and youngest son of Jesse. They lived in Bethlehem and David served his father by tending his sheep. The prophet Samuel invited Jesse and his family to a feast after receiving a divine command to appoint one of Jesse's sons as king. Jesse was accompanied by his seven sons. Samuel looked at all of them to see which ones God intended him to anoint in 1 Samuel 16:6-7 (KJV). He eventually asked Jesse if he had any more sons after exhausting all of those options and having the Lord reject each of them in turn. 'There is still the youngest,' he replied, 'but right now he's minding the sheep. Jesse was commanded to "Send for him" by Samuel. In 1 Samuel 16:11-13, David was anointed Israel's next monarch. He was not descended from King Saul. He did not come from a very privileged background and his family was quite enormous for a young boy. Everything about David becoming king went against social norms and cultural expectations. The Lord, however, picked him. After that life-altering experience, he went back to being a shepherd.

It was through the task of shepherding the sheep that David got the skills he needed for leadership. David's testimony of survival and victory came from a place of isolation. His skills to lead, protect, cover, defend and remain accountable were honed to a divine standard. There are times, in each of our lives, where we run when we are challenged. However, we must confront our challenges with courage. David teaches us in 1 Samuel 17:34-35 that potential is discovered during a crisis. David was protecting his father's sheep. Keep in mind that the sheep did not belong to him at all. David had no aid in the pasture, but he learned from his experiences in the pasture. Fighting the lion and the bear was unfair, but necessary. Just like David, we must find our strength in the challenge.

There are situations in life where we find ourselves in a fight that is questionable, but the experience prepares us for our next. This causes me to raise the following notion: What seems to not be your fight, can actually turn out to be the place of your assignment. David had no clue that his conflicts in the pasture were a part of the preparation for his destiny. This says to us that our private battles will prepare us for public affirmation. Our preparation stages often occur in moments of obscurity and isolation, but our purpose is exposed when we become visible. Isolation is defined as being separated, alone, or in solitary. Another word that can be attributed to isolation is the state of being "hidden." We must embrace the moments of being "in hiding" in order to embrace the necessary strength for our appointed time of revealing. Once you are revealed, there is no retraction. God used every challenge that came by way of David's experiences to confirm that He was God's choice. In that same regard, what we do not understand now will be explained later. Furthermore, what is not disclosed now will be exposed later. Jesse presented the sons based on what he saw or felt. David was never given an opportunity, but became the choice. This, in turn, says to us that the people that man chooses to ignore God will empower. Jesse did not see David's faithfulness, but the Lord did. This is why the Lord chose him instead of the others. Oftentimes, what is not seen in development is recognized and later acknowledged in destiny. It is critical for those of us, who are called by God, to understand that we should not allow your performance to be based on acceptance.

When you consider your life, in light of who and what you did not have, where do your thoughts actually land? If you can be honest, they do not arrive at a place of resolution. Isolation can feel like we are being stripped. The human side of us likes to feel as if we are in control. When we are stripped, we feel defenseless in so many areas. Nonetheless, it is in the aspect of "stripping" that we are being clothed, covered and conditioned. Was it really isolation, rejection, or abandonment? Or were your experiences an ordained move, by God, to work a divine plan? Could it be that we question the process when it was really God's intentionally ordained plan? So many people are waiting for closure when they have already received their conclusion. Stop wasting time waiting for validation when you have been given justification. Free yourself, so you can become your authentic self!

NOTES

Chapter 2

Ignore the Noise!

Nehemiah 4:6 (KJV) - So built we the wall; and all the wall was joined together unto the half thereof: for the people had a mind to work.

We can learn a lot about leadership, perseverance, and faith from Nehemiah chapter 4.

First, we should not cower in the face of dissent. When Nehemiah and the Israelites set out to rebuild the city walls of Jerusalem, they met significant resistance.

Their adversaries made many attempts to demoralize, scare them off, and ultimately attack them. The Israelites, led by Nehemiah, did not give up. They had faith in God's presence and power to deliver them from their adversaries.

Second, the fact that we are imperfect should not deter us. A man of weakness and timidity, Nehemiah was. He doubted his ability to steer a huge reconstruction effort. Nehemiah's frailty, however, was used by God to teach him humility and dependency. Nehemiah matured spiritually and expanded his influence as a result.

Third, we must not be reluctant to try new things. Nehemiah understood that repairing Jerusalem's walls was a risky business. He knew it was a gamble, but he was prepared to accept it because he thought it was the right thing to do. He was confident in God's ability to safeguard the Israelites and himself.

It is important that we are not afraid of hard effort. Nehemiah and the Israelites toiled tirelessly throughout the night and day to repair Jerusalem's walls. They had the requisite drive and dedication to put in the demanding work required to succeed.

In the conclusion of this narrative, worshiping God should not make us uncomfortable. As they worked to restore the walls, Nehemiah and the Israelites continually gave thanks to God. They understood that it was His grace that had enabled them to carry out their goals. They wished to show their appreciation for His help by paying tribute to Him. This goes to show us that God may use the unlikeliest of individuals to do extraordinary things, as is demonstrated in Nehemiah 4. If we put our faith in Him and put in the effort, He will help us triumph over any difficulty.

Nehemiah never shifted from his assignment to satisfy the desires of his enemies. According to Webster's dictionary, the word Ignore is defined as "refusing to acknowledge or intentionally disregard." Nehemiah refused to allow his focus to be shifted from his assignment in order to inquire about the news that was presented to him from the mouth of his enemies. This is a practical lesson for us that can give us a tremendous level of insight in regard to our everyday life. Curiosity can sometimes become a distraction that can lead to destruction.

Maintaining your concentration is crucial since it lets you do the following:

- **Gain greater effectiveness and efficiency in your work.** When you dedicate your whole attention to just one task at a time, you can finish it fast and accurately. This can help you get where you are going more quickly while reducing stress.

- **Improve your judgement.** Maintaining concentration allows for more logical and clear thought. You will be able to consider all of your options and make a well-informed choice.

- **Concentration on the task at hand is a necessary precursor to successful knowledge acquisition.** You can increase your competence and open up new opportunities by doing so.

- **Enjoying life more and get more done.** To be happy and productive, you need to be able to give your attention to the things that matter most to you. This has the potential to make one's life happier and more prosperous.

Concentration is the key to achievement in any field. Training your concentration will help you reach your objectives.

- **Know what sets you off.** Knowing what makes you lose focus is the first step toward blocking it out completely. In what ways do you find it difficult to maintain concentration? Understanding your triggers is the first step in creating boundaries to guard your focus.

- **Manage the world around you.** Having some say over your physical surroundings can help you focus more easily. This necessitates locating an area free of distractions where you can get some things done. This includes putting your phone on 'Do Not Disturb' (DND), taking time for yourself, and eliminating smaller time-consuming distractions.

- **Establish limits and boundaries.** It is crucial to establish limits with those in your life who are always trying to derail you. This involves conveying your desire for their help while also making it clear that you will not tolerate any attempts to undermine your plans.

You must keep your end goals in mind. Remember your goals when you feel overwhelmed or distracted. You must continually ask yourself the following questions: What exactly am I in pursuit of?

What makes this a priority for you? Maintaining concentration and drive requires regularly reminding oneself of one's goals. A focused mind speeds up momentum. An unfocused mind delays your productivity. The reality is that you will never see your future without focus!

Nehemiah was supported and endorsed by the King. This is what kept him focused. Nehemiah did a work because he was trying to assist the people. When you are not supported, it will put you in a place called pretending. Sanballat wanted a position for recognition, but Nehemiah had an assignment to secure the peoples safety. Nehemiah knew he was doing a "good work" because he saw progress and not because someone verbally said it. The king released

Nehemiah to rebuild the wall. A release is constant support with consistent reassurance. Nehemiah's presence was questionable and his assignment was intimidating. This says the following to us: If you allow people to shift your focus, they can alter your outcomes. You cannot give your ear to a voice that does not carry credibility. The weight of the voice that covers you is greater than those who try to discredit you. Do not let people talk you out of what you have been called into! Behind every person there is a personality. Behind every gift there is a grace. We must learn how to confirm the personhood of an individual while guarding their grace.

Sanballat and Tobiah criticized Nehemiah and then they conspired against him. In that same regard, people will conspire against your progress when you exceed their expectations. There are people that want to see you fail because they lack the ability and the courage to do something that has never been done before. You must stop internalizing criticisms and embrace confidence in your capabilities. Conspiracies and deconstructive criticism come to dismantle your focus.

What you see is what you produce! In order to do what you have envisioned or complete what you have started, you must strategize, analyze and prioritize. Starting anything without a plan leads to stagnation, but a plan in motion leads to satisfaction or surprise outcomes. When you are focused and busy without distractions, the results come quicker. Let resistance become your motivator to "Go Harder!" Center your focus on the crucial details. Why? Success is found in the details. Nehemiah's project was completed in 52 days. How was this done? When opposition came, Nehemiah did not allow distraction to become an interruption. There are several instances, in our everyday lives, where we are faced with layered challenges and measures of adversity. We allow obstacles to weaken our motivation and resolve when moving forward. In all actuality, our obstacles should become our motivation to keep moving forward. You must refuse to come down from what is working for you and give your attention to nothing. Stay focused and planted! Do not become a slave to the enemy's plots when you are free to produce.

Nehemiah stayed committed to his mission of repairing the walls of Jerusalem because he understood that doing so would ensure the safety of the people. He was unfazed by his opponents' jeers and threats. Nehemiah understood that the success of the wall's reconstruction depended on the participation of the people of Jerusalem. He divided the individuals into work parties, each of which was responsible for a certain segment of the wall. This not only sped up the work, but also provided them with a sense of pride in the project they were contributing to. Nehemiah persevered despite many obstacles during the wall's reconstruction. Even though his rivals were trying to stop him, he worked nonstop. The Jerusalem wall was reconstructed in just 52 days.

Sanballat and Tobiah strategized in order to distract Nehemiah. Instead, Nehemiah ignored the irrelevant and focused on what was working. When we lose our focus, we have the tendency to walk away from the plan. Walking away or deviating from the plan only gives strength to the plots of the enemy. Nehemiah's position was "on the wall" and not near the wall. Connecting to the assignment is an enhancement to embracing the purpose for the assignment. We refrain from embracing the fullness of our call because we are afraid of the vulnerability that comes with connection. Connectivity requires joining, linking, togetherness, communication and accessibility. We are reluctant to extend ourselves to these connecting points when we have been placed in a compromising position and faced with disappointments.

Nehemiah was encouraged in his work to repair Jerusalem's walls by King Artaxerxes of Persia. Nehemiah was his cupbearer, but he gave him a leave of absence, letters of safe passage, and letters to the governors of the provinces west of the Euphrates River so that he may rebuild the wall. Nehemiah was able to go to Jerusalem to demand materials for the reconstruction project thanks to the letters he received. Nehemiah received financial backing from King Artaxerxes. Nehemiah was able to buy timber and other construction supplies thanks to the money he was given. Moreover, he gave Nehemiah soldiers to guard the construction workers. This is why it is essential to have the proper endorsement coupled with legitimate blessing. When you depart to engage a specific undertaking, it is the blessing that will lead to your success. Progress, in any form, without blessing or endorsement is short-lived and cannot be sustained in the long-term.

Nehemiah could not have completed the reconstruction of Jerusalem's walls without the backing of King Artaxerxes. Nehemiah could not have made the trip to Jerusalem, bought the necessary materials, or protected the workers from harm without the king's permission. Faith in Nehemiah and confidence in the significance of repairing Jerusalem's walls led King Artaxerxes to lend his support.

- Nehemiah was his cupbearer. Distressed at news of the desolate condition of Jerusalem, Nehemiah obtained permission from Artaxerxes to journey to Palestine to help rebuild its ruined structures. He was provided with an escort and with documents that guaranteed the assistance of Judah's Persian officials. The king dispatched letters to the governors of the districts west of the Euphrates, ensuring Nehemiah a safe journey.

- To help Nehemiah with the cost of lumber and other construction supplies, he gave him financial support.

- He sent soldiers to Nehemiah to help guard the construction workers.

King Artaxerxes support of Nehemiah is a reminder that no matter how difficult things may appear, God will always be there to back us up. It is important to consider that where there is purpose, there will always be provision. The question then becomes: What happens when you set out to accomplish a goal, but stop due to opposing forces? You must evaluate and then make strides to accumulate what is needed to go forward. Allow your freedom to become a place of accessibility. As you journey forward consider the following:

- **Reevaluate your objective.** Is it still something you wish to accomplish? If not, it may be time to establish new objectives.

- **Break your objective down into smaller stages.** This can make the task appear less daunting and more feasible.

- **Determine the forces that are preventing you from achieving your objective.** Once you have identified the opposing forces, you can devise strategies to overcome them.

- **Find a support network.** Having people who support you and believe in you can make a significant difference.

Resistance can bring about so many feelings in our humanity.

We must honestly find out what is causing the pushback. Finding out where the pushback is coming from is the first order of business. Is the opposition coming from within you, from others, or from both? The first step in overcoming opposition is identifying what's causing it.

Secondly, recognize how you are feeling. Recognize your emotions when you encounter obstruction. Feelings of anger, frustration, or even fear are normal. These feelings are natural responses to difficulty.

Avoid taking it to heart. Keep in mind that opposition is not necessarily motivated by hostility. People often fight change because they are fearful of what will come next. Sometimes they are hesitant because they are scared of what might happen if they give in. If someone rejects your help, try not to take it personally.

Keep your sights set on the prize. Facing opposition can cause one to lose focus. Nevertheless, remember why you started and what you want to accomplish. Just keep pushing forward and remind yourself why you are doing this.

Seek assistance. Do not be reluctant to seek assistance if you find yourself unable to overcome opposition. Discuss your feelings with someone you can confide in, whether that is a friend, family member, therapist, etc. They are a source of help and advice.

Trust in your own abilities. Have faith in yourself and your capacity to prevail against adversity. Having confidence in oneself increases the likelihood that you will stick with something until you succeed.

We learn a lot about perseverance in the face of opposition from Nehemiah chapter 4. Furthermore, there are some additional insights that will assist your in developing the resolve to pursue the completion of an endeavor or goal amid resistance.

Expect to face challenges. There will always be naysayers whenever you set out to construct anything. This is especially true if the task you are undertaking is worthwhile and significant. Nehemiah anticipated opposition to his plan to restore Jerusalem's walls and prepared accordingly. He was prepared for the challenges ahead and confident in his ability to overcome them.

Do not give up when faced with difficulty. It is simple to quit up when you are met with resistance. Always remember having an opponent does not mean you have failed. In fact, it is typically a good indicator that you are doing something well. Nehemiah overcame many challenges and never gave up. To ensure the safety of the people, he persisted through the challenges of building the Wall of Jerusalem.

Collaborate with others. When you have a team behind you, building anything is a breeze. Nehemiah was aware of this; therefore, he enlisted the help of the Jerusalem populace in the wall's reconstruction. This sped up the process and made them feel more invested in the project. Having individuals who believe in you and are eager to help is crucial when you are trying to overcome obstacles.

Get God involved! There will always be moments when you feel like you cannot take on the opposition, no matter how well prepared you are. Praying for God's intervention is crucial at this time. Nehemiah prayed to God for assistance since he knew he could not complete the wall's reconstruction on his own. God granted

Nehemiah's request to rebuild the city wall of Jerusalem. If we are willing to endure in the face of opposition, as we are reminded powerfully in Nehemiah chapter 4, we can overcome any difficulty.

Chaos has the ability to expose us to our potential. If Nehemiah had not seen the condition of the walls, he never would have been compelled to undertake this risky endeavor. In turn, this speaks not to just a matter of faith but the willingness to undertake a risk. Sometimes, it is a "risky move" that can put one in a safe place. Although encountering chaos is often unpleasant, it can also present a unique chance for personal development. We can emerge from the turmoil stronger, smarter, and more capable than ever before if we can learn to embrace it and see it as an opportunity to find our potential.

Chaos has the potential to shake us up and make us try something new. When things get chaotic, it forces us to think creatively and quickly. This can aid in the identification of latent skills and potentials. It can help us focus on what matters most. When our lives are turned upside down, we learn to prioritize what really matters. We can better prioritize our actions and achieve our goals with this information in hand. Chaos has the potential to propel us into action. We can either do nothing when anarchy ensues or we can take steps to improve the situation. Taking decisive action can improve our sense of agency and the world around us.

Chapter 3

Positioned In A Place To Save!

Genesis 50:19-20 (KJV) – *And Joseph said unto them, Fear not: for am I in the place of God? But as for you, ye thought evil against me; but God meant it unto good, to bring to pass, as it is this day, to save much people alive.*

Joseph was one of the 12 sons of Jacob. His father gave him a colored cloak because he loved him more than anyone else. His siblings, filled with envy, sold him into slavery. He was brought to Egypt, where he became the steward of one of Pharaoh's officials, Potiphar. Joseph was imprisoned after Potiphar's wife unsuccessfully attempted to seduce him and fraudulent accusations were made against him. As a result of his skill in interpreting Pharaoh's dream, he was appointed superintendent of Egypt. He prudently rationed the nation's food supply in readiness for a famine.

During the dearth, Jacob's sons traveled to Egypt to beg Joseph for food. They did not recognize him, but once he was assured that they had been reformed, he happily identified himself. Joseph extended an invitation to his father and siblings to settle in Egypt. The account appears in the Old Testament (Genesis 37, 39–45, KJV).

The dreams Joseph had made his brothers envious. The Bible describes two dreams that Joseph shared with his brothers. In Joseph's first dream, he and his brothers were both sheaves of wheat, but his sheaf stood proudly while theirs bowed. In a second dream, the sky's celestial bodies all bowed before him. Joseph's dreams are a preview of how God would use him beyond where his brothers considered him to be. In the same instance, people make the mistake of classifying you without being aware of the cause for which God will use you in the future. Always remember, when purpose is driving the process, the proof is in the results.

Joseph's brothers interpreted his dreams as portending his eventual triumph over them. They resented the idea that their father's favorite son, Joseph, was also their superior, and they were envious of his status as the favorite son. Because of their envy, Joseph's brothers sold him into slavery. They believed Joseph's dreams were over, but God had other intentions. Joseph was promoted to second in charge in Egypt over time. When his family fled to Egypt from the famine, he utilized his status to aid them. Joseph's outcomes show us that what is destined will manifest. The narrative of Joseph is a powerful example of how God can work in the midst of adversity to accomplish His good will. Joseph's brothers may have been jealous, but they could not stop him from becoming the great leader he was destined to be.

Joseph was chosen to save them, but they only saw the position but not his purpose. There are times where people cannot accept the reality of who you are destined to be. In each person's life, there are certain undeniable characteristics that point to the inevitable gifts, talents and abilities that will lead an individual down a certain path. People have expectations of you not based on your actual purpose, but their expectations of you are constructed by their preferences and perspectives. Just because they see you in a certain light, does not mean they actually know you. People can be envious of your place and miss the purpose of you being placed. The sobering reality is that there are people that are in close proximity to you, but they cannot bear to see you become anything past where they are. You should not dilute who you are to become what they want you to be. You have to recognize who you really are. Some individuals fail to reach their full potential because they do not recognize their innate value. Subsequently, you should refuse to accept the limitations of people's short-sighted projections with information and self-fulfilling prophecies concerning your life's outcomes.

Joseph finds himself in a situation that was not God ordained, but God allowed. God will use the plots of the enemy to work a plan. There are times in life where our potential is challenged. However, it is the fires of adversity that challenge our potential and perfect us. Jealousy, according to the bible, is as "cruel as the grave," but the grave cannot hold a person that has purpose.

Jealousy has the potential to be fatally cruel. It has the potential to eat away at our insides, causing feelings of inadequacy, anger, and resentment. It can also cause us to act in ways we come to deeply regret. As a result, envy is a potent feeling that may wreak havoc on our wellbeing. It has the potential to shatter friendships, professions, and even spark physical conflict. Although jealousy may be a part of circumstances that surround us, we should be aware that it will not stop us! God's plan prevails over the inconveniences that were caused by man. Joseph's uncomfortable and unfair life placements were what qualified him for the position he would appointed to by Pharoah. The dream that was perceived as a fantasy, by his brothers, became a reality. What Joseph saw in Pharoah's dream is what positioned him to be a solution.

God will raise up a person when there is a need. If someone is needed, God will make them visible. Psalm 113:7 (NIV) declares that God "lifts the needy from the ash heap" and "raises up the poor from the dust." This shows that God can and does utilize the unlikeliest of people to bring about His plans. The famine presented a challenge for Pharoah, but it presented Joseph with an opportunity to construct a new reality.

Joseph was put in charge of both the home of Potiphar and the jail. Scripture calls Joseph a "young man of great personal beauty and physical strength" (Genesis 39:6, KJV). To show his appreciation, the Egyptian captain of the guard Potiphar put Joseph in charge of his household. Potiphar quickly came to respect Joseph for his administrative acumen.

Potiphar's wife, however, developed romantic feelings for Joseph and attempted to seduce him. After Joseph turned down her advances, she falsely accused him of rape. Because of his anger, Potiphar had Joseph locked up. There is an important lesson that we can take away from this situation. Because of the favor seen by Potiphar it became a physical attraction to Potiphar's wife. Joseph's assignment in life was more important than allowing a "flesh move" to dictate his movement. We must never confuse the parameters of our favor. When the favor that is on you becomes attractive to those individuals who are outside of you, you must quickly discern an assignment from an attachment. In the practical sense, there are some of us who have ended up in a relationship, cycle, or situationship that was simply an assignment. It is imperative that you do not cross the line! Take a lesson from Joseph. Leave in order to lead!

Joseph maintained his reputation as a wise and capable man even while behind bars. He quickly won over the jail warden and was given responsibility for the inmates. Joseph's confidence in God did not waver even in the face of his many difficulties. He refrained from taking revenge on Potiphar's wife or the jail master. He did not brag either about his dream-reading skills. God rewarded

Joseph's obedience, and he was able to use his position of authority for the greater good.

Joseph had a great deal of knowledge and skill. Joseph was a smart and effective leader. He ran Potiphar's household and the jail like clockwork and did so fairly and equitably. He was especially helpful to Pharaoh because of his ability to decipher dreams. Joseph had a heart of compassion. He did not try to enrich himself by his position. Instead, he put his abilities to use by assisting others.

We may have been placed in a position with limitations, but it does not determine the dimensions of the grace that we have been given. God gives us a grace that exceeds our current circumstances. God's grace is greater than our difficulties. The grace of God is "sufficient for all things" according to 2 Corinthians 12:9, NIV). God's grace allows us to transcend intentional limitations that have been set in our way. This is encouraging to each of us because we should not allow our place to control our space!

The pit was temporary. Potiphar's house was an avenue. The prison was his point of acceleration and the palace was the place of his ascension. When Jospeh's family comes to Egypt to escape the famine, he is in a position to save them. This shows us that what is destined will manifest. The struggles, difficulties, and unfair situations we face have a way of building us to become who we are today. It is through these types of situations that we learn to be resilient via them. You develop resilience when you have to overcome obstacles. This entails developing the resilience necessary to recover quickly from setbacks and carry on when going through difficult times.

They are great for shaping who you are as a person. Challenging situations help you grow as a person by making you face your vulnerabilities head-on. This has the potential to make you a better, all-around person. They teach you to be grateful for what you have. You gain a deeper appreciation for life's blessings as you navigate through adversity. One possible outcome is more thankfulness and happiness. They encourage spiritual development. You may find yourself praying to God for guidance when life's hardships become too much to bear. You can strengthen your belief in God and advance spiritually by doing this.

Further considerations of how adversity and injustices might shape us:

They can teach us to feel for others' situations. Experiencing adversity helps us empathize with those who are suffering through it as well. Because of this, we might grow kinder and gentler.

They have the potential to make us more modest. It is common to develop a haughty attitude after achieving some measure of success. However, setbacks can teach us valuable lessons about our own fallibility and help us develop a humbler disposition.

They can teach us gratitude for those who back us up. We learn who our true friends and family members are when we face adversity. Those that are there for us through thick and thin are the ones we can always count on.

Joseph's dreams were a force that propelled him into his future. In that same regard, we must allow our purpose to be the driving force. Facing those people who have caused us issues can put us in the same mindset as Joseph. He poses the question, "Am I not in the place of God? Do you see me where I am? You meant evil against me, but God used it for my good to save many." People may have tried to get rid of you, but your survival was far beyond them. It may be a process to release feelings of resentment or enacting forgiveness, but freedom is for the sake of your deliverance.

Chapter 4

Confrontation VS. Confirmation
Deliverance from Rejection

There were many factors that led to Jeremiah's rejection. To begin with, many people disagreed with his message. The people of Judah did not take well to his prophecy that they would be conquered by the Babylonians. Second, Jeremiah was a young man who was not held in high regard by Judah's political and religious elite. They felt threatened by him and sought to have him silenced. Third, Jeremiah was a negative prophet whose words typically spelled disaster. He was disliked because he gave the people of Judah little reason to be optimistic about the future.

Some of the reasons why Jeremiah was disregarded include the following:

1. He was labeled a "false prophet" by Judahite elites. They said he was just making stuff up, not quoting from the Holy scriptures.

2. The residents of his hometown of Anathoth made murder threats against him. They disliked him because he had spoken ill of the city in his prophecies.

3. The king of Judah put him in jail. The monarch did not want Jeremiah to preach to the people because he was terrified of his message.

4. The citizens of Jerusalem dumped him into a cistern. They wanted to put an end to his prophesying about the city and were furious at him for doing so.

Jeremiah continued to serve God even after being ignored. Even when it was risky, he kept prophesying. Despite this, he was sent into exile in Babylon. He never stopped serving God. His prophecy came true when the Babylonians conquered Judah and carried off its inhabitants. Jeremiah's message, however, included a message of optimism for the future as well. The return of the people of

Judah to their country was another of his prophecies that came to pass.

It is clear from the events surrounding Jeremiah that God's prophets are frequently disregarded. However, that does not make what they are saying false. In fact, it is a good indicator that what they are saying is crucial. The word that Jeremiah brought to the people of Judah served as a warning and prepared them for the impending exile. When we are rejected, his message serves as a reminder that God is still faithful.

The spirit of rejection is a spirit of oppression. It robs you of serenity and happiness. The definition of oppression is mental pressure or distress. Consequently, if the spirit of rejection is an oppressive spirit, you can think of it as a strategy employed by the adversary to press you into the moods or emotions that prevent you from experiencing freedom and the presence of God's love. Does this indicate that God has abandoned you? According to the Psalm 136, God's affection will never fail. You must therefore be able to distinguish between what you experience and what is true. This is the result of comprehending the spiritual strategies employed by the adversary.

The Spirit of Rejection is tactic used by the enemy for the purpose of deception. When you realize that the spirit of rejection tells falsehoods about God's love and your value, you can begin the process of being liberated. In spiritual warfare, the adversary employs the fortress of rejection. The spirit of rejection provokes feelings of insignificance in you. It collaborates with the spirit of an orphan to make you feel unwelcome. Typically, the sentiment of rejection begins at a young age. The oppressive spirit searches for parts of your intellect, will, and emotions — your soul — that yearn for love, acceptance, and self-worth.

God Made You to Long for Love and Acceptance. The Enemy warps it. God's intention is to be the fulfillment of this desire. However, the enemy distorts every human's aspirations. This stronghold of rejection calls your identity into question and suggests that you are not completely a part of God's plan. It conflicts with the essence of sonship.

There are known expressions of the Spirit of Rejection:

- You feel hopeless. There do not appear to be any words of encouragement that can liberate you from this sensation of rejection.

- You feel excluded from conversations, as though you are an observer unable to participate.

- You feel that life's opportunities have passed you by and that it is too late to take advantage of them.

- If those in authority do not acknowledge your accomplishments, you feel shunned.

- You begin to feel envious as you compare your circumstances to those of others.

- You were not given a fair opportunity in life, as evidenced by feelings of envy and comparison coupled with rejection.

- You feel compelled to prove yourself while simultaneously believing you will never measure up.

Do any of these emotions ring true for you? There is spiritual warfare occurring within your mind, will, and emotions. This spiritual stronghold is cunning, but it cannot compare to the power and transformative love of Jesus Christ. Rejection can also be passed down through generations. Today, we can see that the mentality of rejection is frequently inherited through the following personality traits such as neglect, selfishness, physical, psychological, and sexual violence, use of illicit drugs, repetitive unfavorable language and messages, broken families, and marriages, and unable to assume parental responsibilities.

Through generational curses, oppressive spirits seek opportunities to attach themselves to you. Each of us is born with the desire to be adored. However, if we do not experience it as God intended, the adversary will attempt to accuse you of bringing these circumstances upon your family line. Then he subtly searches for openings where spiritual oppression can take hold.

Rejection has the ability to destroy a person's existence like few other things. The number of people who have experienced rejection is, sadly, staggering. If we wish to become all that God has created us to be, then overcoming rejection and its effects is crucial and essential.

Many individuals who experienced rejection and abuse as children develop unhealed emotional wounds as adults. Rejection results in emotional wounds, which, if not cleansed and released, fester and become spiritual wounds (such as unforgiveness, envy, blaming God, jealously, etc.). These spiritual wounds leave us vulnerable to the invasion of evil entities, who relish the opportunity. The objective of the adversary is to equip us with emotional baggage and negative sentiments against one another, ourselves, and God.

Rejection bears many fruits that can differ greatly from person to person.

Among the most common signs of rejection are:

- Both infants and adults are susceptible to rebellion.

- In order to be accepted, fabricated personalities (being someone you are not) are prevalent.

- Overcompensation of strengths and "people-pleasing."

- The propensity to reject others so that you are not the first individual to be rejected.

- A tendency to constantly question whether a person welcomes or rejects you.

- The need to be welcomed by others and to participate in everything.

- Self-pity in which a person feels sorry for being alone.

- Incapability to tolerate correction or constructive criticism.

Rejection creates an environment in which you are love-starved or do not belong.

- A disposition to blame God. Why did God create me so small?

- A pride that exclaims, "How dare they reject me!"

- Personality with strong opinions and the need to be correct about everything.

- Feelings of worthlessness, mistrust, and despondency.

- Seeking parental approbation indicates that your identity is dependent on what they think of you.

Rejection can inspire envy, jealousy, and even hatred. Because your identity depends on what others perceive of you, you fear confrontation. A person who has difficulty confessing errors or receiving constructive criticism has an underlying rejection issue. How is this known? Because their identity, who they are, is dependent on their ability to be correct about everything. For the same reason, stubbornness may also have its origins in rejection. They must be correct, or else they feel meaningless, because "who they are" (their identity) is contingent on their correctness. This also relates to opinionated personalities, who are always there to tell you everything they know about something, despite having little or no actual knowledge to speak from.

Then there is performance orientation and drivenness, certain variants of OCD, etc., in which a person bases his or her identity and sense of self on how well they perform at something in life. When we base our identity on our performance or being right about something, and when we falter, it is a blow to our identity.

Those who struggle with rejection may also become "fixers"; a "fixer" is a person who is eager to inform everyone else how they should be doing things, despite frequently lacking the necessary knowledge or experience. Such a person attempts to be the Holy Spirit in the lives of others, despite having neither the authority nor the right to do so. They find their identity in resolving other people's issues, and they adore it when others seek their assistance or counsel.

The reality is that we were designed to be adored, accepted, and valued. Rejection is an anti-Christ spirit because it opposes our God-given nature. Rejection deprives a person of the love and acceptance for which they were intended. When we rely on others or even ourselves for affection and acceptance, we set ourselves up for failure and the harm of rejection. God alone is trustworthy as the source of our identity.

Self-rejection is an additional component of this puzzle. Self-rejection occurs when an individual rejects themselves. They are unhappy with who they are. This frequently results in self-hatred, self-resentment, etc. It is frequently associated with self-unforgiveness if the individual has made grave mistakes that they profoundly regret. As much as it stings when others reject us, self-rejection can be equally damaging.

Then there is perceived rejection, which occurs when an individual interprets something as rejection when it is not. For instance, "Why is that person refusing to coming over to speak with me?" When the person may not be attempting to reject you, but is simply too shy to approach you (or anyone else) at the time. Because the purpose of a spirit of rejection is to make us feel rejected, people who possess such spirits may tend to perceive rejection. Those who believe that God is always furious with them typically struggle with feelings of rejection.

Perceived rejection can also lead an individual to believe that God has rejected them.

The source of rejection is surprisingly straightforward: the damage caused by rejection is the consequence of a misplaced identity. When we base our identity on someone or something other than what God's Word says about us, we expose ourselves to the destructive effects of rejection. Many of us base our identities on the opinions of our parents, instructors, and peers. This prepares many children for Performance Orientation relationships later in life, as their parents condition their affection based on their grades or performance.

What or who defines your identity? Is this your duty? Is it what your parents believed or believe about you? What do your peers think of you? Is it your performance in the workplace? How much cash do you possess? Is it how well you perform in school? What do you believe about yourself? Is it your physical strength, fitness, or height? Will these characteristics continue to characterize you after death? Rejection and overcoming rejection are all about identity and what you use to define yourself. The secret to overcoming rejection is to resolve identity issues.

Suppose you determine your identity based on what your parents think of you. Due to the fact that they are the source of your identity, any indication of disapproval from them will cause pain. When we base our identity on what we believe about ourselves or on what others believe about us, we are essentially entrusting that individual with our identity. Only God is capable of accurately determining who we are; we are incapable of doing so ourselves. Therefore, it is of the utmost importance that we comprehend the person that God has created in us and who we are as new creations in Christ Jesus. We were never intended to live apart from God or to derive our identity from worldly objects. When we base our identity on what the Bible says about us, we become virtually immune to rejection. As long as we do not base our identity on what another individual thinks of us, we can become immune to the pain of rejection.

The closer a person is to you, the more devastating their rejection can be. Because you look up to and rely on authority figures, they have the ability to inflict severe harm. When parents say, "I'll love you when you get good grades," they are frequently communicating rejection to their children. Conditional love results in feelings of rejection and ties such as performance orientation and a need for achievement. Whether one loves or despises a person does not protect them from rejection. Are you defining yourself by what others think of you? Does their approbation provide meaning and purpose to your life?

Age plays a significant role in a person's susceptibility to rejection. Children are particularly susceptible to the negative effects of rejection because they are still forming their identities and discovering who they are. Peers cause significant harm in school. It does not matter if you are too short, too tall, too obese, too skinny, or if you have brown eyes when you should have blue eyes; children will pick on you! Insecure children can be extremely spiteful, causing harm to their peers through rejection. Why? As a result of not basing their identity on the proper things. They do not know who they are or what they are destined to be, so they make themselves feel better by putting down other children. If they knew who they were in Christ, the narrative would be very different! They would also assist other children in discovering their identity and vocation.

Is it conceivable for a child or even a grandchild to reject you? Yes! No one is immune if they base their identity on what others believe of them. You can be 100 years old and still be hurt by a caretaker's rejection. As I mentioned previously, it is crucial that our identity, who we are, is based on what God's Word says about us. When this occurs, we become essentially immune to the debilitating and damaging effects of rejection. God promises to never leave or forsake us, so when our identity is based on what He says about us, we can rest assured that He will never reject us. All it takes is one positive word to dispel any negative comment. My conviction is to strongly suggest that you do not have to "live in" where you were left, but instead take a risk to "move from" in order to "move into" your next place.

God is calling you to a greater place than where you currently are. God will lead us somewhere better than where we are right now. If you feel stuck or unfulfilled in your current situation, take heart in this promise of hope and encouragement. The meaning of the expression "a place that is greater than where we are" varies from person to person. Some people may be starting over in a new location, either professionally or physically. For others, it may refer to a more inward or emotional destination, such as a closer walk with God or a more meaningful sense of life's purpose.

The promise of a better place, whatever that may mean to you, is a sign that God has something wonderful in store for you. He is aware of your abilities and eager to see you develop them to their fullest. Do not lose faith if you are unhappy with where you are in life or the dynamics of certain personal connections. God has a bigger plan for you, and He will eventually call you there.

Our experiences contrasted with Jeremiah's narrative says to us that resistance is confirmation of your assignment. Many people may fight against our growth for many reasons. It is possible that some people are threatened by our success, while others are simply terrified of change. Some people may just disagree with us on our aims or approach.

Resistance, for whatever cause, can be disheartening and irritating. On the other hand, it also has the potential to educate us. One thing it can show us is how challenging it can be to make a change. Some people will always be resistant to progress, no matter how positive it is. This is because transitions can be disorienting and unpleasant. It has the potential to test our assumptions and ideas as well.

Second, we can learn the value of persistence through encounters with resistance. We must persevere in the face of opposition if we are to realize our objectives. We have to be resilient and keep going even when things get tough.

Third, resistance can instruct us to be receptive to criticism. If someone is fighting against our advancement, we should consider their arguments. Even if we disagree with the resistance's motivations, we can still benefit from hearing their perspectives.

Ultimately, the lesson of resistance is that we are not alone. Some folks are not the only ones trying to make a difference. We can accomplish our goals and overcome obstacles if we work together.

Here are some concrete lessons we can learn from confronting our resistance head on:

- **It has the potential to help us develop patience.** It is easy to give up in the face of opposition to our growth. But with persistence, we will finally win them over.

- **It has the potential to make us more empathetic people.** It is crucial to investigate the motivations of those who oppose our growth. We may use this information to better understand their objections and devise strategies to overcome them.

- **It has the potential to foster innovation.** When others oppose our progress, we must think outside the box to discover solutions. This can aid our efforts in developing novel approaches to the challenges we confront.

In the end, obstacles present themselves as learning opportunities. Our efforts to bring about positive change can only be strengthened by the lessons we take away from the difficulties we encounter along the way. Being met with opposition from others has the potential to fortify our resolve and the resolve to succeed. When we encounter difficulty, we often feel like giving up. However, if we are truly committed to achieving our goals, we may use this opposition as fuel to propel us forward.

Opposition or resistance has the potential to infuse our pursuits with renewed zeal. When we encounter opposition to our growth, it can fuel our determination to succeed even more. It is possible that we will feel pressured to prove our doubters wrong or to demonstrate our abilities. This could serve as the spark we need to keep going. The benefits include increased resilience. In the face of adversity, we toughen up and develop the ability to bounce back. Despite difficulties, we are taught to pick ourselves up and keep going. This toughness can be crucial in reaching our objectives.

Opposition may help us concentrate better. We sharpen our focus and determination in the face of adversity. We pick ourselves up when we fall and learn to keep going no matter what comes our way. This concentration can be crucial for continuing forward and accomplishing our objectives. The experience of encountering opposition from others can teach us important lessons. It has the potential to make us more committed, sturdy, and goal oriented. These traits may be necessary for us to succeed.

Just because a person rejects you does not mean other people will refuse to receive you. What others refuse to receive will be embraced by others and will benefit them. Failure to get acceptance does not reflect negatively on your character. It only indicates that you and the person that rejects you are not good match. People who accept you for who you authentically present yourself to be are hard to come by.

When experiencing rejection, it can be helpful to remember the following:

- **Ignore the tone; it has nothing to do with you.** It is possible that the person who rejected you did so for reasons that have nothing to do with you.

- **Do not use it to judge yourself.** Your value does not rest on other people's opinions of you. You add value to the world, and there are those who will recognize this.

- **Do not rush the recovery process.** Feelings of hurt and disappointment are normal responses to rejection. Feel your feelings, but do not ruminate on them.

Rejection has the potential to prevent you from coming into contact with anything that is harmful. The feeling of being rejected can be excruciating, but it can also present an invaluable educational opportunity. You can gain valuable insight into who you are and what you want out of life via the experience of being rejected. It also has the potential to assist you in preventing similar errors in the future.

For instance, if you are turned down for a job by a potential employer, the reason may be that you do not meet the requirements for the position, or it may be that you do not mesh well with the culture of the firm. This may be a trying time, but it also presents an excellent opportunity to gain some very useful knowledge. You may get a better understanding of both your strong points and your weak points, and you can also get a better understanding of the qualities you seek in a job. Using this information, you should be able to find work that is a better match for your skills and interests.

In a similar vein, if you are rejected by a potential relationship, it may be because the two of you do not have enough in common with one another. This may be a trying time, but it also presents an excellent opportunity to gain some very useful knowledge. You can gain an understanding of your own emotional requirements while simultaneously gaining an understanding of what you desire from a mutual partnership rooted in reciprocity. Using this knowledge, you should be able to choose a person who is more compatible with you in the long run.

Rejection is not necessarily a negative experience in every circumstance. It is possible that this is a sign that you are heading in the correct direction at times. For instance, if you are not accepted into a school that you really wanted to go to, the reason may be that you are not prepared enough for the amount of academic challenge that the institution presents. While it is possible that this will be an upsetting experience, it also has the potential to be a very instructive one. You will be able to gain insight into the academic areas in which you excel and those in which you struggle, as well as gain knowledge on the steps you need to take in order to increase your chances of being accepted into a better school in the future.

The way you respond to rejection will ultimately determine whether you view it as a positive or negative experience. Rejection can be viewed as a beneficial learning opportunity provided that the individual takes what they have experienced and uses it to better themselves. On the other hand, if you let yourself become disheartened by rejection, then the experience can be a bad one.

We must release the pressures of rejection. The mind can only contain so much. Freedom is a release from bondage. Just because you have moved forward, does not mean you have moved on. Genuinely moving on, releases you to move in and live in the now and not the past. An Exit is not always leaving. There are some people that Exit to Return and some that Exit to Enter. A Disconnect creates the opportunity for a Connection to the catalyst for your next move, which is freedom. Freedom comes from within.

Jeremiah was validated by God, but rejected by men. Some people walk away from their assignment because of rejection. When you walk away from your place of assignment, you reject God's investment and hurt the people that you are assigned to. When you are not accepted, you tend to question your self-worth. Validation should be louder than rejection. Both in psychology and in one's own personal growth, the concepts of validation and acceptance play a vital role. There is a distinction between the two terms, despite the fact that they are frequently interchanged with one another.

The act of recognizing and agreeing that the thoughts, feelings, or experiences of another person are credible is what we mean when we talk about validation. It involves acknowledging that their feelings are genuine and reasonable, despite the fact that you may not share the same sentiments. Validation is a powerful tool that can help people feel understood and accepted in their experiences and perspectives.

The act of accepting someone or something in their current state, without passing judgment on them or offering criticism, is the process known as acceptance. It implies admitting that someone or something is different from you, while at the same time understanding that their differences do not make them flawed or undesirable. The process of acceptance might be challenging, but it is necessary for developing healthy relationships and leading a happy life. Acceptance is crucial.

We should consider that there are some primary distinctions between validation and acceptance:

- A statement that recognizes and agrees that the views, feelings, or experiences of another person are valid. Without passing judgment or offering criticism, accepts someone or something in their current state.

- Can assist individuals in experiencing a sense of acceptance and understanding. Can assist in making individuals feel more appreciated and cherished.

- Can be a potent instrument for the development of wholesome connections. The process may be challenging at times, but it is necessary in order to lead a happy life.

To summarize, validation refers to having an understanding, whereas acceptance emphasizes appreciating the individual. Both are necessary for maintaining healthy relationships as well as making progress in one's own life.

Validation and acceptance are illustrated by the following examples:

The following is intended to serve as validation: "I understand that you are currently feeling angry. That is a very reasonable way to feel.

Acceptance: "I accept that you and I are both unique individuals. That is not a problem.

Validation: "I understand that you are experiencing a sense of melancholy. That must be a trying experience.

Acceptance: "I acknowledge that you are going through a challenging time at the moment. I will always be here for you.

It is possible for people to feel understood, respected, and appreciated by employing the notions of validation and acceptance, which are both significant in their own right. Think about how you can apply these ideas in your life whether you are seeking ways to enhance the quality of the relationships in your life or to further your own personal development.

Like Jeremiah, what you contain is much larger than where you are. Jeremiah realized that the Word in his belly was the Investment to an Enhancement. He did not allow his meltdown to become a breakdown. Releasing the word to the people was an enhancement to their lives. You must not allow your emotions to control your actions. You cannot be effective if you continue to live in your hurt. A lot of times people mask their weaknesses by overcompensating with their strengths. Quitting can be a Choice, but not a Good Option. Perception is becoming aware of something through the senses. Your perception is not 100 percent accurate, but your discernment is accurate. Discernment is the ability to judge well. Discernment protects, exposes, and explains. If you want to walk in "true freedom," as you go forward in life, you must see by way of discernment. Your life should progress from its current position and not remain stationary.

Set objectives. Having distinct objectives gives you something to strive for and keeps you motivated. Ensure that your objectives are specific, measurable, attainable, relevant, and time bound.

Make a move. It is simple to get stuck in a rut, but taking action is the only way to move forward. Even if it's a minor step, taking action will bring you closer to achieving your objectives.

Be persevering. There will be setbacks along the path, but it is essential to remain steadfast and continue moving forward. Never abandon your objectives, regardless of how difficult they become.

Gain insight from your errors. Everyone makes errors, but it is essential to learn from them. Reflect on what went wrong and how you can avoid committing the same error in the future when you make a blunder.

Commemorate your achievements. It is essential to celebrate your accomplishments, regardless of how small they may appear.

Celebrating your accomplishments will keep you motivated and propel you forward.

Find a support network. Having a network of peers, family, or a mentor can be extremely beneficial when attempting to advance. Support from others and encouragement can make a significant difference.

Moving forward from where you are and avoiding stagnation requires effort and commitment, but it is possible. Do not allow a city to limit you from reaching a state. Do not allow a country to stop you from reaching the world. Some possess an anointing for the nation's but cannot operate past their current location. Do not cry about being accepted by man when you are included.

The key is to stop thinking about what you are experiencing and start thinking about what you observed. Recognizing the possibility instead of the disaster is the key to finding a solution. Only this very instant exists in your experience. You can never be sure of how things will turn out. You can only live in the now, in this very instant. This is the only instant you have any say over. Both the past and the future are beyond your control. At any given time, you can decide whether you love or despise your life. You can also choose to disregard or squander it. You can direct your attention wherever you like in this very moment.

You can only experience life in the now, so choose wisely and make the here and now your ally, not your foe. Thinking too much about the past or the future might cause stress. While little stress can be beneficial, chronic stress and an inability to stay in the present can have serious consequences for your mental, physical, and emotional well-being. Living in the moment has been shown to lessen stress. Pay attention to the times when your thoughts drift away from the now and into the past or the future. Mindfulness training can help you live in the here and now.

Every second you spend on Earth is a blessing. There is no way to know how long your life will last. Knowing that you should be grateful for every second of your life is crucial. Since you have no control over the future, you should make the most of the present.

Neither the past nor the future are habitable places to be, so the only place to be is right now. The present is too precious to waste. Do not let worrying about the past or the future prevent you from appreciating the here and now. Each time you have on this earth is precious; take full advantage of being alive while you can. You can't be prepared for "life," as the saying goes," as stated by English musician, singer, and songwriter John Lennon

Things rarely go according to plan. Though it will aid you in the long run, future planning will not immediately enhance your quality of life. Even with careful preparation, the future may not go as planned. It can improve your odds, but plans do not always come to fruition the way we imagine or hope they would. The future, like anything else in life, is uncertain. Present moment awareness is all you can really count on. Whether you like it or not, this is the truth.

- How frequently do your plans not turn out the way you want them to?

- When things did not go as you had hoped, how did you respond?

- How did you respond to the situation—with compassion or anger?

Both success and failure are planned for. The majority of the time, your best-laid strategies will fail. Sadly, it is inevitable. It is impossible to anticipate every eventuality in advance. Besides being unachievable, it is bad for your health. The more you prepare for something, the more disappointed you will be if it does not materialize. Adopting a more adaptable approach to planning would be helpful. Planning is helpful, but not if it causes you to miss out on enjoying the here and now.

You will be happier if you learn to appreciate the here and now. To increase the amount of joy and sunshine in your life, practicing mindfulness can help. Right now, is a precious gift that you should not waste. Living in the present has been shown to increase happiness. The importance of living in the here and now cannot be overstated. It is possible to miss out on today's splendor if you spend too much time planning for the future. Just enjoy the here and now and be content with it.

Do not spend too much time dwelling on the past or the future. Keep your focus on the here and now. Maintaining equilibrium between in-the-moment experiences and future preparation and retrospective analysis is essential. The only thing you have is right now, so make the most of it and live in the now.

NOTES

Final Thoughts ....

Freeing yourself opens the door to healing yourself! It is difficult for anyone to take criticism well, but for the very sensitive individual, it may be heartbreaking. Some strategies employed by the highly sensitive to avoid criticism include people-pleasing, self-criticism (before the other person has a chance to), and avoiding the criticizer altogether because of their heightened sensitivity to the effects of criticism.

While criticism may be painful, it need not be debilitating. How comments are made determines whether they are constructive or deconstructive. Constructive criticism identifies shortcomings and offers solutions (e.g., "Be sure to check your blind spot before switching lanes"). Negative comments that do not offer any suggestions for change (e.g., "You are doing it all wrong!") are examples of destructive criticism.

Do not jump to conclusions.

When we are criticized, our natural reaction is to defend ourselves. Criticism, even when well-intentioned, can have the opposite effect and make us feel rejected, activating our fight-or-flight responses. When we respond quickly out of anger or other strong feelings, though, we often make hasty, unwise statements that we come to deeply regret. Try not to jump to conclusions and respond right soon. Get some distance from the circumstance so you can figure out how you are going to deal with it. Do not blurt out anything until you have collected your thoughts a bit more.

Do not think in absolutes.

Many people battle black-and-white thinking, which means that they might go from considering themselves a big success to a catastrophic failure based on their most recent experience. This kind of thinking inhibits individuals from perceiving themselves as an integrated, balanced whole, made up of both positive and bad characteristics. Maintain focus on the here and now and ground your thoughts in reality. Once an extreme belief has been recognized, the next step is to challenge it by asking,

"Where is the evidence that I am the worst person on the planet?"

Promptly inquire.

The smallest bit of criticism can be taken the wrong way. Make sure you comprehend all that has been said to you by asking clarifying questions. This is especially vital if the critique is ambiguous. If you want to make sure you are getting the point of feedback right, try paraphrasing it and asking the sender, "Am I understanding this correctly?"

Find the glimmer of truth.

Every criticism, it is said, has a grain of truth. At the very least, the truth of how that one person views you is embedded in criticism. Just because you give yourself permission to keep an open mind does not mean you have to accept everything you hear or do anything with it. People we encounter in life frequently serve as mirrors, reflecting back to us aspects of ourselves that we cannot see clearly. Try to take this setback and turn it into an opportunity for growth.

Decouple your emotions from the truth.

Do not put too much stock in your emotions. Emotions are just that—emotions—and not facts. They do not always provide you with an accurate picture of what is going on in the world. People have trouble seeing the big picture when they are being criticized since it brings up uncomfortable emotions like humiliation, embarrassment, frustration, rage, inadequacy, hopelessness, etc. Consider whether your emotions stem from the here and now, from your history, or from your future worries.

"Letting go gives us freedom, and freedom is the only condition for happiness. If, in our heart, we still cling to anything—anger, guilt, or possessions—we cannot be free." ~Thich Nhat Hanh

It is simple to say, but a lot tougher to put into practice. We all make mistakes occasionally, whether it is yelling at a buddy, acting destructively to oneself, or slacking off at work. And those errors frequently result in intense feelings of shame. Shame. Self-condemnation. Humiliation. If neglected, these emotions can cause stress, sadness, and anxiety disorders, according to counselors and life coaches. Not exactly the recipe for happiness in life! Fortunately, you can avoid these harmful effects and lead a happier life if you learn how to forgive yourself and choose to let go of the guilt.

Why Should We Forgive? Why Is It Such a Big Deal?

It takes conscious effort to choose forgiveness when you have unfavorable feelings against someone or yourself. Prior to forgiving, you could feel the following negative emotions: guilt, shame, self-condemnation, humiliation, as well as resentment or bitterness.

Your well-being depends critically on your ability to forgive errors or wrongdoings. Learning to forgive "helps people hurt less, experience less anger, feel less stress, and suffer less depression," according to Dr. Frederic Luskin of Stanford University. People who practice forgiveness report much fewer stress-related symptoms like headaches, dizziness, backaches, and upset stomachs. People often mention improvements in their eating, sleeping habits, vitality, and overall wellbeing. You can let go of negativity and concentrate on a more promising future by forgiving both yourself and others. It also gives you the chance to strengthen bonds with your loved ones.

Why Is Forgiving Oneself So Difficult?

We punish ourselves for past transgressions far too frequently, as if we could somehow "make up" for the wrong that we have committed. Every day, we go about our business feeling inferior. We label ourselves as failures and bad people. We are bound by our history and harbor sorrows and resentments. And even if no one else is aware of our private suffering, the unfavorable feelings we experience eat away at our happiness and sense of fulfillment in life.

According to therapists and life coaches, it is most difficult to forgive oneself. Not the one who betrayed you, pal. Or the father who did not stand with you, even the heartbreaker from your past. Why? because you are familiar with yourself and regularly interact with yourself. Oh, right.

1. Discuss it.

Silence can be fatal when discussing the past. So, stop acting and pretending. Talk about what is ripping you apart inside and release yourself from the shackles of holding it all inside. To a trusted friend, mentor, or counselor, express the feelings you are experiencing. Being open and vulnerable about who you are—the good and the bad—is the first step in forgiving someone. So, say what needs to be said.

2. Be truthful to yourself.

We frequently believe that "If I just pretend it never happened, maybe it will all go away." Nice sounding, but untrue. Decide to stop living in denial and start acting. Tell the truth about your mistakes and the effects of your actions. Write down in the precise actions and behaviors that are upsetting you.

3. Recognize its limitations.

You will have failures in life since you are a flawed being. Admit it. Sometimes, you'll do others harm. You'll feel guilty. It is a natural consequence of existing in a fallen planet. The choice is yours, though. Either you accept your history for what it is and are free to go on and enjoy the present, or your past will keep you stuck in a cycle of guilt and shame. Don't skip out on self-acceptance because it's essential to your emotional wellbeing!

4. Let go.

Do not cling to your guilt. You do not need to defend your prior choices or try to vindicate yourself. Putting the past to rest entails burying it and renouncing the right to self-criticism. Both a choice and a process, forgiveness. It involves making the decision to stop devaluing or disliking oneself and start seeing yourself as a valuable human being. Getting it out there is one of the first stages in letting go.

Creating Reasonable Expectations

Examine the standards that you and others have for you. Are they wholesome? Or are they improbable? You might just need to make a few small adjustments to your way of living if you constantly fall short, no matter how hard you try. Healthy expectations are not exhausting and overpowering, but rather attainable and satisfying.

Agreement with Oneself

Now is the time to agree with yourself to...

Live in the present and let the past go. Stop criticizing yourself for an event that occurred two, five, or ten years ago. Stop letting guilt and shame dictate your thoughts and actions. Recognize and value who you are as a person... regardless of your screw-ups.

Unhealthy Attachments are rooted in unhealthy decisions. Life is both awesome and terrible at times, that much is true. If you want to succeed in life, decide what you want and go get it. No one would say that life is completely trouble-free. Life stinks, we all know it and confess it. What worries me is that rather than breaking free of the rut they have been in for years, many people "choose" to give in to it.

Here's the deal: I emphasize the word "choose" because, ultimately, it is our decision that determines the outcome. We make the most of life by making the most of it. It is normal to feel helpless, annoyed, and even hopeless when we are struggling with difficult problems. Nothing unusual here. We could just bemoan our plight instead of asking, "Why not?" One option is to pretend the issues do not exist, betting that they will go away on their own.

Choosing to act on one's own desires is the essence of living. I have found that the old cliche about following your passion is true: if we do not act on our enthusiasm, our lives have little meaning. Do not listen to the critics; pursue your dreams, nonetheless. In the face of uncertainty, one should "fail forward" and "learn from their mistakes." Do not let the expectations of others or your current situation hold you back. It is okay if you do not know what you are living for in this world. Not many people do. No need to rush or pause. Never give up!

Let me demonstrate some elementary arithmetic:

Action + Reaction = Positive Outcomes

You better believe it. What determines your success is not your situation but rather how you choose to deal with it. Your decision-making process, your reaction to the incident, and your ability to learn from it are all potential factors in the outcome you experience. Always look for the hidden meaning and check the assumptions. If you feel the timing is right, trust your gut and act, even if it is just a baby step. Keep at it, even if it is just a little bit each day, and you will get there.

Freedom is being liberated, fulfilled, and living the life you have always desired. But how many are willing to perform the necessary actions? Living a life full of passion requires effort, but when done correctly, it does not feel like a strain. Which to Listen to: Heart or Head? How do you know what your true desires are? You could consult your intellect, but that red, beating organ in the center of your chest will provide a more accurate response. Your intuition knows things that you did not even know were possible. It is your guide, and if you follow it, it will take you where you need to go. Do not expect miracles when you listen to your intuition; rather, anticipate whispers and subtle hints.

It is far too easy to turn to others for guidance in life. At some point, you must factor in your heart and start following your own path. Listening is as easy as placing one's attention in the heart. If you have not already, you should take a 15–20-minute break, close your eyes, and sit silently while feeling your heart. Accept whatever may arise. You may experience a variety of lingering emotions in your body and psyche. Acknowledge them, gain insight from them, and leave them alone. If you do not know how to handle the emotions that arise, your progress will remain stagnant.

You were born to do what you love, to experience life to its fullest extent, in whatever manner brings you to life. You can make a livelihood doing work you enjoy as long as it adds value to people's lives. No crystal orbs exist. Nobody can ensure your prosperity. Your journey will likely not resemble anything you imagined it would. Remember that our life's journeys operate in enigmatic ways at all times. Life is a journey, and portions of that journey may involve passing through storms that generate a great deal of perplexity. However, this does not mean that you are the storm, nor does it mean that the storm will not pass.

Instead of maintaining a steady trajectory, running in all directions is a common method of evading the storm. You exert a great deal of effort, but you end up exactly where you began. You must cultivate a realistic perspective of reality. If you desire freedom, fulfillment, and to do what you enjoy, you must be realistic and courageous. To make this work, you must have an accurate view of reality, and the only way to reach a point where you begin to taste success, freedom, and fulfillment is by learning from those who have gone before you, taking action, and learning from your errors. If you are serious about living the life of your dreams, you must start to become more self-aware and actively pursue your passions. You do not need to be certain about your passion; simply begin doing what interests you, and that will lead you to the next activity, and then the next, until you awaken your purpose.

Change your attitude to reflect on the person you aspire to be. Your attitude will determine whether you progress or regress. It is heavily influenced by your beliefs since your beliefs determine your decisions. Your beliefs are primarily based on your past experiences, including what others have said and done to you and what you have concluded about yourself as a result. Consider the veracity of statements made to you as a child. Examine your accomplishments and your environment, and review your past actions to determine if they align with the accusations.

You are more knowledgeable than you believe. Stop underestimating yourself by saying "I do not know"; instead, say "I will figure it out" and ask "How can I do this better?" As part of your self-development journey, you are able to seek assistance and interact with the appropriate resources so that you can grow, gain knowledge, and prepare for future challenges.

Allow people to enter.

Do not be afraid to reach out to those you feel comfortable with and share your struggles with them. When you believe in yourself enough to reach out to others, trusting that you are deserving of their support, you will attract opportunities you never thought possible. Take risks and be truthful, and life will surprise you.

Consider challenges as opportunities.

Life will always present you with obstacles, regardless of how hard you strive to avoid them. Instead of avoiding them, learn to view them as opportunities to improve your current situation. Obstacles exist to teach you something new. The hidden message will only be revealed to those who exert great effort to surmount them.

Acknowledge and learn from your blunders.

Do not be overly critical of your own actions. It is inevitable in life to make blunders. You will grow to genuinely adore them. Even though we try to avoid making errors as much as possible, I know that they are our best teachers for personal development and growth. If there is something you truly desire, you must be willing to take opportunities, put in a lot of effort, and never give up trying to get it.

You need to make sure that your goals are in line with your core beliefs. It is good to let go of your old principles and start over on your path if you find that, as you progress through life, your priorities, and ideals shift, as we all know is natural and expected as we age. If you are aware of what it is that you truly desire, you will be better able to judge when the time is right to back down and go on, and when it is best to fight for what you believe in. You have the ability to triumph over the limiting ideas that prevent you from achieving your full potential and generating happiness in your life. The first step is to make the decision to cease giving them power and to start seizing fresh chances instead.

Circumstances are defined by Dictionary.com as: "a condition, detail, part, or attribute, with respect to time, place, manner, agent, etc., that accompanies, determines, or modifies a fact or an event; a modifying or influencing factor." In a spiritual sense, it can be defined as the circle in which you stand. We should not remain stationary. We ought to be progressing from glory to glory according to Colossians 3:18.

Each time a person meticulously reviews, renews, and refreshes their circumstances, they are forced to experience them again. We should not resurrect our current dilemma. We must search for solutions and ways to transcend our conditions whatever their nature may be.

However, in chronic circumstances, this may necessitate a shift in perspective.

If we believe there is life and death in the power of the tongue, and the Bible states that there is, then there is. Calling the circumstances yours, would be a grave error. The World English Bible translation of Proverbs 18:21 says, "Death and life are in the power of the tongue; and those that love it (i.e. - he/she/they) will eat its fruit." Whatever you say belongs to you. Give God your circumstances. Rise above the enemy's deception.

According to 1 Peter 5:7 in the Amplified Bible it states, "Cast all your cares on Him, for He cares for you." This is the query. Who would you rather have monitoring your situation? God or you? Cares, anxieties, worries, and concerns appear to be the results of your circumstances. According to the conclusion of Mark 11:23 in the King James Version, "…..He shall have whatever he desires." Second, do not disregard or deny that God is greater than your circumstances. When we have been struggling with a problem for a long time, we have a strong tendency to let the adversary convince us that we must accept it. There is an age-old proverb. I am not certain who first penned it, but it is potent. It says, "Do not tell God about your major problem. Tell your dilemma that God is great."

Abandon perfectionism

Life is not flawless. You are fallible. Occasionally, you will fall short. Your children's hair will be tangled, your home will be untidy, and you will arrive at work wearing a shirt with wrinkles. Occasionally, you will have to order pizza instead of preparing a home-cooked supper. You will have a cluttered kitchen island and mounds of mail staring you in the face. Perfectionism can be a powerful motivator, but its benefits diminish swiftly. Consider how many people dwell on the issue of having a child out of wedlock. Many people find themselves unable to appreciate what came forth. Nurture and move from the places of your past mistakes and leave the past in the past. The past combined with strides towards perfectionism rapidly robs you of the time, energy, and focus you can devote to what is truly essential in your life and career. Occasionally, it is best for one's own equilibrium and well-being to settle for mediocrity.

I am not suggesting you cease caring. Do your best, but do not let the pursuit of perfection destroy the good that is presently happening in your life. When you find yourself worrying about doing something perfectly, take a step back and consider whether good enough is sufficient. Practice caring less about minor details and concentrating on the big picture.

Get away from the fixed cost fallacy.

When you have invested a great deal of time, resources, or energy in something, it becomes difficult to let go. Even when it is objectively in your best interest to alter your course of action, such as when you are in a bad job or relationship, this can occur. You think to yourself, "I have already invested so much in this. "How could I possibly leave now?" If something is not succeeding despite your best efforts, it is sometimes best to swallow the bullet and walk away. Instead of doubling down, consider how you got on your current path. Consider whether you would have continued if you had known what you know now. If the answer is no, why do you continue to repeat yes?

Cease deliberating.

Occasionally, we all get caught in a mental loop. We lie awake at night contemplating all the things we should have said or done that day, our misgivings, and the decisions we wish we could reverse. We frequently struggle with the notion that we overlooked something that should have been apparent or that we lacked an answer that should have been straightforward. These thoughts play in our minds like an endless loop. Does this ring a bell? It can be very challenging to let go of misgivings, worries, and negative past experiences. However, by dwelling on these matters, we are tormenting ourselves. By focusing on the things, we cannot change, we deprive ourselves of the energy and time we could devote to the things we can change. Instead of fretting about what was out of my control, we have to reframe our thoughts to focus on what we can influence. What are you able to gain from these experiences? How can you be proactive in the future? By forcing ourselves to retrain our thinking, we were able to break the cycle and begin having healthier thoughts. If you are a worrier, you should begin to record your thoughts. How many of them are within your control? How can you reframe your thoughts and concerns to be more kind to yourself?

Consider your prospective self.

Many of us are significant procrastinators. This is a dangerous practice, particularly when deadlines are tight. Procrastination is insidious because it enables us to avoid something in the present at the expense of our happiness in the future. Remember that your future self is responsible for the tension caused by your procrastinating present self. By kicking the can down the road, you sign up for tension in the future, typically more than if you had simply completed the task now, before the deadline approaches. Consider your future self the next time you sense the urge to procrastinate. Consider what they would have wished you did today and put yourself in their position. They are pounding on the window, imploring you to complete the assignment immediately, rather than waiting until it falls into their lap. Pay attention to them.

Make room for the inconsequential.

Occasionally, a number of minor concerns begin to accumulate. A large volume of correspondence is received. You are confronted with a series of deadlines that are too close together. No matter how often you sort through the collection of mail on the counter, it seems to continue to grow.

Individually, each of these items is a minor inconvenience. But when they all bother you simultaneously, they rapidly become overwhelming. Sometimes there seems to be so much to do that you cannot possibly complete it all, so you become paralyzed as your to-do list grows longer and longer. This exacerbates the issue, creating a vicious cycle. Resolve anything that can be resolved immediately. If you allow minor tasks to accumulate, so begin creating space so you can clear away minor items as you can. Stay on top of the simple tasks to avoid becoming overburdened.

Look ahead, not behind.

It is far too common to neglect this and dwell solely on the negatives. How much time do you spend dwelling on the job you did not get, the promotion you were passed over for, or the poor evaluation you received? How much of this time could you devote to learning, development, and achievement?

We all have anchor points, whether they are mistakes we have made, missed opportunities, or regrettable judgments we wish we could reverse. If you are always gazing behind you, you will stutter as you move forward. When you let the past anchor you, you prevent the future from flourishing. Consider your anchor points while taking a step back. Create a list of past events that are holding you back, then destroy the list. Next, create a new plan: jot down a list of constructive actions that will propel you forward. By embracing the future and looking ahead, you can shift your focus from what cannot be altered to what will be altered in the future.

Run one's own course.

The old proverb states, "Comparison is the thief of joy." Comparing your daily existence to the highlights of another person's life is a surefire recipe for disappointment. We believe that we are not competent, intelligent, or successful enough. We focus on the accomplishments of others and ponder why we are unable to replicate them. We exert greater and greater effort because we view life as a race with only one winner. The reality is that life is essentially a marathon, not a sprint. Even completing is an achievement. Consider only your own species. You may not begin in the same location as another player. You may not possess the same tools. It is possible that you were not born with the same quantity of stamina. However, you have the chance to run the greatest race for yourself. Stop glancing to the left and right to see how quickly others are running, and do not allow others to define success for you. Instead, concentrate on the progress you can make, the obstacles you can overcome, and the goals you can establish. You may be quicker or slower than others, but what matters most is that you complete the marathon on your own terms.

Accept the possibility of being evaluated.

Sometimes we hold back to feel safe or to defend ourselves, but there is a cost to remaining silent. There is a risk involved when putting yourself out there. You expose yourself to the scrutiny of others. However, taking this risk is what allows you to refine your leadership skills and evolve. Growth does not occur without the risk of being judged, but by accepting this risk, you allow yourself to participate in the dialogue. Start small if you frequently find yourself withholding your opinions or contributions. Choose one activity per day that is outside of your comfort zone. Perhaps it involves sending an email to a superior or speaking up in a large meeting. You will become more confident and have a greater impact in your role and function the more you put yourself out there.

Recognize and accept your history. Acknowledging the past is the first thing you need to do in order to start moving on with your life. This entails coming to terms with the fact that your past took place and that it has had a role in shaping who you are today. However, this does not imply that you are required to let your history determine who you are today.

Forgive yourself as well as the people around you. Keeping bitterness, wrath, and guilt inside of you will do nothing but leave you mired in the past. If you want others to forgive you for your mistakes, you must first forgive yourself. This does not imply that you have to forget what occurred; however, it does mean that you have to let go of the negative emotions that are preventing you from moving forward.

Gain wisdom from your past errors. Everyone is prone to making errors. However, the most vital thing is to take something useful away from them. You should not allow your past mistakes define you, but you should learn from them.

Concentrate on the here and now. The past is finished with us, and the future has not arrived just yet. The only thing that can be trusted is what is happening right now. Therefore, make the most of the here and now and try to savor every moment of your existence.

Accept and enjoy your independence. After you have conquered your demons and set yourself free from the past, you will be able to fully appreciate your independence.

This means that you should live your life according to the rules that you set for yourself and not let anything hold you back.

It is not simple, but it is possible to free yourself from the burdens of the past. It is possible to break free from the confines of the past and welcome freedom into your life if you are prepared to put in the effort required.

Failure is often the result of a fixed mindset, the belief that one's strengths are fixed, finite, and barely open to development. This individual considers their positive and negative traits to be mostly predetermined at birth. While they generally acknowledge the significance of education and training, expanding their minds and envisioning a bright and radically different future is often just out of their reach.

A growth mentality, on the other hand, is one that is always striving to develop and enhance one's latent abilities as well as those that have been cultivated through experience. Those of us who adopt a growth mindset believe that with hard work and perseverance, we can develop and hone abilities we did not have before. Those who truly embrace a growth mentality do not only think this way; they act accordingly. The famous quote attributed to Henry Ford goes as follows: "Whether you believe you can do a thing or not, you are right."

Ford realized that the only thing that can stop you from accomplishing something is the conviction that you cannot. A rigid outlook may have occurred to him as a potential source of misery. People who have a growth mentality are less prone to dwell on setbacks and more likely to take criticism constructively and utilize it to improve. A person with a growth mentality is someone who is eager to expand their knowledge. As a result, they will be open to new experiences, confident in their abilities, and motivated to succeed. Because of this, people may be more willing to consistently explore solutions, which might help them be more creative.

When you adopt a growth mindset, you are less likely to let self-limiting ideas get in the way of realizing your full potential and acting in ways that are consistent with your core values. With this kind of liberty, anything may be achieved. It gives you the strength to try, fall short, and try again.

Those who have tasted such liberty are certain that they can affect the lives of those around them. They do not have a fixed worldview.

A growth mindset, however, may be cultivated by repeated effort and focused attention. To begin, you need to have faith in your abilities. Try using a mantra or some other daily reminder. Believe that you have the power to make all the necessary adjustments. It may take some effort, but the benefits of development and success are well worth the effort themselves.

Do not put the blame for your failures on outside sources. You must accept that you are in charge of your own destiny and must maximize your own potential. Therefore, the next time you see yourself placing blame, pause, reflect on what you can learn from the experience, and then move on.

Those interested in making a difference also need to be naturally inquisitive. Be amazed at how little you know. Accept this sensation as normal. It is not something to be ashamed of or afraid of, but rather something to be excited about. Asking inquiries and trying to learn more is a great way to follow up.

Give yourself permission to fail. It is important to attempt and fail, even if it makes you uncomfortable, because it's the only way to learn. Rejection is a key to development. Every setback is an opportunity to learn and improve for the future. You do not need me to list all the notable people who bombed out early in life but eventually rose to prominence and became inspirational figures in their fields.

Learn to thrive in situations when you are not completely at ease. Many of us use our comfort zones as safe havens, where we can relax without worrying about making mistakes. On the other hand, without obstacles there is no room for improvement. Grow by challenging yourself.

You should not be too focused on the end outcome. Yes, outcomes are often what matters, but do not forget to celebrate your successes along the way. Self-appreciation for a job well done can keep you going when the going gets tough. When things get rough, it is time to rely on the process.

Keep an eye out for becoming envious. Think, "I'll use their success as a model for what I want to achieve," rather than, "Boy, do I wish I had achieved what they have." The former pushes you to achieve more, while the latter holds you back. You can use adoration as a compass to help you reach your goals.

Finally, avoid letting your pride prevent you from making positive adjustments that could improve your life. When you adopt a growth mindset, you will be challenged to move beyond your current level of competence and confidence. Ego hates it, but if you listen to it, you will end up just like everyone else. Challenge your own ego, limiting beliefs, and assumed restrictions if you want to flourish and excel.

The brilliance and success of others will not frighten someone with a development mindset because they are focused on improving themselves rather than protecting themselves. They will be more prone to look up to others, take cues from their actions, and be motivated by the achievements of those around them. This is how you will Free Yourself!

REFERENCES

Holy Bible: The Amplified Bible. (2015). Zondervan. (Original work published 1965).

The Holy Bible: King James Version. (1769). Oxford: Oxford University Press.

Holy Bible: New International Version. (2011). International Bible Society. (Original work published 1973).

www.ingramcontent.com/pod-product-compliance
Lightning Source LLC
Chambersburg PA
CBHW071207160426
43196CB00011B/2221